I0504234

THE

HOMEBUYING

BLUEPRINT

Save *Huge Cash* with Real Zero Down Buying for a Home or Investment Property

By

Jason Powers

Copyright 2019 by Kindle Direct Publishing- All rights reserved

It is not legal to reproduce, duplicate or transmit any part of this in either electronic means or printed format. Recording of this publication is strictly prohibited.

This is dedicated to all the people out there who take action on their dreams!

Table of Contents

Introduction

Cheers on purchasing this e-book that will inform you on how to truly save a fortune as a real estate owner.

If you're a first-time buyer or seasoned investor, by adding these few simple, often overlooked steps in your home buying process you will avoid paying any down payment. Also, demolishing the excessive interest banks charge, getting you an outstandingly low monthly payment. Your mortgage can even be paid off in a fraction of the time compared to most owners.

The barrier to entry for home buying is REAL! Most people feel overwhelmed hearing the old narrative that, "You have to save up a lot of money to put a down payment." An example of this is when the media mongered on the mortgage crisis in 2008 blaming faulty financing policy. Thus, in the mind of many people; it's very difficult and even scary to start the process of getting qualified to buy a home.

But knowledge is power! This short simple read will give you honest, formidable insights based on principals that only the best and brightest use to finance property today.

I've been in this industry helping people buy homes for over 24 years, I started when I was 16 years old under a mortgage broker, climbed the latter to loan officer in my early 20's and an investor by my late 20's.

I've looked at every strategy on homebuying and the one I am going to share with you today is what works best to get you in to your own home with none of the cost most people are used to hearing about. This is crucial information on the biggest purchase most people make in their whole life.

After reading this book, plan on having much more confidence and options in the whole buying process.

I will be showing you how to use secret tools given by all mortgage bank's that most realtors or mortgage officer don't have a clue about. These same tools are the one's often used by savvy buyers who know the value of holding your hard-earned cash in a saving account that pays interest instead of a mortgage account that charges it. You'll see in this book how it is better math to finance zero down and have non-traditional payment schedules to beat the interest to 0%.

I've used this strategy both for myself and clients to buy 1000's of homes over the course of my career. Now is the time for you to learn this knowledge so you can take informed action on the most important issue of the process…Which is, "Where is the money coming from?"

In this book, I am going to show you, step-by-step, how to fund your dream with zero down and save tons of cash on interest. Read it, take note and start shopping for that home sweet home.

Chapter One: The Dream of Owning Real Estate

Owning a home is a keystone of wealth...It possesses both financial affluence and emotional security.

– Suze Orman

Truly, owning a home is synonymous with living the dream! Did you know that approximately 35% of adults in western countries do not own their home? In America that's almost one hundred million people who do not have that benefit. Although, as a youth in school most of us are taught that owning your own home one day is a part of living a good, successful and comfortable life in modern society.

Naturally the vision to own property and have comfy shelter persists and grips even tighter for those who have a growing family or for those of us who simply see the incredible value of owning real estate.

The General Consensus

Most people believe the societal narrative that says you have to save up for a down payment and if you can't do it you can't afford to buy a home and you should wait longer and learn how to save.

For those under the general consensus that feel it's just out of reach because it's "So expensive" or they say to themselves, "I have to save for years to do that!" While saving up is a strategy that can work, it is also quite a load to carry and requires a lot of resources, time, and sacrifice. If you've done it and you're ready to buy, good on you! Just read on for a lesson on keeping that money in a safe place that is always easily available while still cutting your payment and interest more than people who put huge down payments.

You're about to learn the simple strategy of buying a home for less than buying a lease/rental. You'll learn how to keep any large sums of cash where it belongs…In your personal bank account!

Whether you have saved up for a family home or are just eager to buy one or multiple home for investment, this guide will be your shining light in the darkness of all the typical obstacles that are generally expected that keep one third of the population out of homeownership.

Stepping Out of The Box

Now that we recognize that the broad thoughts on homebuying are leaving a lot of people in the cold or cramping families who need big money for down payments and closing cost which depletes most family's cash savings.

It's time to adopt a new mindset that puts buyers in the green and makes banks pull more of their own weight. Which they will happily do, provided you have the knowledge to ask the right bank for the right program. This bit of knowledge can open the door for millions of buyers who have good credit and income but no savings for hard, out-of-pocket costs like traditional homebuying: The 100% financing option!

I will show you how this option will cover every single penny that's needed to get you the keys to your dream home, making it much cheaper than getting into a rental property even potentially cheaper on the monthly payment of a rental as well.

That's where we come in and inform you on how to use this program to finance the down payment and closing cost. We'll also talk about what banks do 100% financing and how to set yourself up to qualify. You're going to learn how to get ALL your cost covered into a loan that will be paid off in no time.

I will cover in more detail which exact lending institutions work with this program and how you can qualify. It's really a local-based program that is available in all 50 states in the U.S. and other big countries that lend mortgage products. Usually credit unions will have it, some of the big banks, and your mortgage broker will undoubtedly tell you about it if you ask. If your mortgage broker does not know much about it, find a new broker who does.

Chapter Summary

- The dream of homeownership has not been realized by hundreds of millions because of lack of knowledge.

- <u>100% financing can cover every penny in getting into a home making it cheaper than a rental in every way.</u>

- <u>In order to use this zero-down strategy, we must think different than what obsolete financial traditions has handed down and go toward zero-down financing option with inner pride despite financial dogma.</u>

In the next chapter you will learn how to position yourself to qualify for 100% loan programs and where to get them. The trick is to gain the qualification standards for your financial and credit profile at all cost, even if it takes some time.

Chapter Two: Buying a Home in Today's World

The way we see it, real wealth means having the money and the freedom to live life on your own terms.

– Rich Fettke, Real Wealth Network

Realtors get an adrenaline rush when you tell them you're putting your life savings down on a purchase. But if you want to do zero-down to save cash...Well, their excitement goes right out the window. Maybe it's because they see there's a bit more actual work involved. Life is not being easy, as it's not easy for those who can't buy a home because of down payment or credit issues and because of this hang-up realtors have to play their cards close to our chest as far as down payment. More on that later in this chapter.

Granted that 100% of financing programs are not as prevalent these days, but they are available for those who ask and seek it out. If your mortgage broker wants the deal, they'll help you find a lender who will do zero down or you can just as easily find another broker and realtor who will do the work.

If one was inclined, you can go directly to both the mortgage bank/lender/credit union and the home seller on your own without the help of any stuffy real estate pros. Unless of course you're lucky enough to find good agents. Either way just follow this guide as your blueprint then go at it with or without an agent.

Pre-Qualification Documents & Approval Process

"The devil is in the details," here at this stage of the game. Your credit score should be 680 or above (don't be discouraged if it's not, solutions ahead). You should have several credit/trade lines (auto loans, credit cards, department store cards, etc.) accounts that have 2 to 3 years of good payment history. If you don't have that, maybe a close family member or friend who does and believes in you will partner up with you as your buyer. Otherwise, you must get that score as a part of this program.

A Quick Word on Credit and Repair

There are very fast credit repair strategies out there online, some are questionable so definitely do some research before you commit. There is also enough information to develop your own credit repair skills to save money and time. This whole credit repair thing is about commitment and tenacity, so if you want it bad enough and see the value you will find a way to make it happen!

You may be surprised at how much you can delete and repair on your own. You need to look at your total credit profile. In the U.S there are three bureaus that provide credit reporting. There are paid credit monitoring services that are good and accurate for about thirty dollars a month. Or there is a free option at CreditKarma.com which makes it easy to help you dispute online for two of the major bureaus. Also going directly to Experian.com and signing up for their free credit monitoring will allow you to dispute the third one online for a full look at what the bank will see.

Now that you see your credit profile, DISPUTE EVERYTHING negative, you'll be surprised how much will come off and what doesn't can be disputed through the mail with credit dispute letters, and you can easily find templated versions of them online, some are better than others. However you choose do it, the time and/or money spent here will yield huge results that can qualify you for your home and help build your wealth fast.

Income Qualification

Income is the next most important thing when it comes to qualifying for this program. Banks want to see provable income documentation that comes from either your employer or from your records as being self-employed. Whichever one you are determines the next steps.

Employed Earners

Since taxes are taken out and your net income is the qualifying amount shown on your W-2, it's easy to see how much you can afford. That net income reflects on your tax returns as well. Prepare a file with 2 years of taxes at the same current type of job (they want to see job stability, as long as you're in the same industry), 2 months of paystubs, 3-6 months of bank statements and any other financial asset documents such as a savings account, 401k's, IRAs, Money Market accounts, etc.)

Self-Employed Earners

If you have ever tried to apply for any loans especially a mortgage loan this can get a bit tricky for self-employed earners. Here is where our gov't regulation on the banking industry has led to an extortionary strategy against the self-employed/1099 earners who wish to own real estate in our tax system.

Most self-employed people usually will show plenty of losses on their tax returns to avoid paying a hefty tax bill. Rightly so…Why should you have to pay exorbitant tax fees when business owners have dealt with a huge inflation rate and rising cost of doing business everywhere?

However, don't be discouraged you can still do this! But here is the reality that you have to work with; **you must show a qualifying bottom line net income on your tax returns to get financed**. I'm sure you're going to think if you do that, you're going to have to pay a big tax bill. Yes, BUT I have good news … you can get out of tax bills too, in fact people do it every day! Overall, its more valuable to own real estate and work out any tax issues as you move forward.

Tax bills are obstacles you can negotiate, not life enders meant to strike fear into the hearts of people, putting them into a mental fetal position. It should not be a reason you disqualify yourself from ever owning property! Thus, if you want to buy a home on a self-employed income, you want that tax bill at least for just a little during your application process for your home, then you can deal with it as I'll mention below.

The lender for your home will need two years of tax returns showing a solid net income that makes sense with the purchase price of your desired home. *But not to worry* you have options if you've shown a loss for the last 2 years, you can file an amendment to your returns which will show a good qualifying income.

You can amend it back after the loan, but you may be red flagged for an audit if your paperwork is not in order.

Better yet, a humbler and much more effective method to eliminate a tax debt would be to request an abatement from the IRS. They'll waive your tax bill provided you fill out the form with the proper sob story of how you just bought a house and the tax debt if paid could render you homeless with irreparable damage, foreclosure and other huge losses. The more drama the better for them to erase your frivolous tax debt. I've used this strategy to personally eliminate $35,000 tax bills. Look up IRS abatements if you're concerned about or facing tax debt!

It's of much more value to own a property and deal with IRS tax issues later. Tax bills don't show up or affect credit. This is per the new credit laws that state public debts cannot be reported on your credit report due to privacy and legal issues[1].

So, file a good provable income that can be supported with recent paystubs and bank statements which shows you can afford your home and don't let government alphabet agencies and their BS policy stopping people from pursuing their right to life, liberty and happiness!

---

[1] https://www.nolo.com/legal-encyclopedia/irs-may-report-tax-debts-credit-bureaus.html

Which Bank/Lender?

Now that you have a handle on how to present yourself to a lender; making sure your credit and income look good. Search your local <u>Credit Unions</u> (CU) in your state who do 100% financing, they are your best option to start. Their rates are low and 100% financing is somewhat common among CU's.

Also ask your broker about USDA 100% programs if you're not in a big city or would like to buy in a rural zone. If you're in a USDA rural zone or would like to be, you're in luck because buying a home with the USDA 100% program offers low rates and other benefits.

If you're former military and qualify for a VA loan they also provide 100% on a home purchase, ask your mortgage broker and they can help you with that.

The FHA likewise offers the 'Good Neighbor Next Door' loan to teachers, police officers, and other public employees, who may buy a home with just $100 down--not quite 100% financing, but extremely close.

For **investors** who want the super-secret 100% financing zero down on purchasing a rental property, COGO financial will allow 100% financing with a seller financed carry back 2nd mortgage of 10%. Send me an email at Creativefinance4@gmail.com and I'll get you all set up for zero down deals on investment property and make sure the seller pays all the closing cost too! More on that in the next chapter.

Chapter Summary

Again, don't let a realtor or a mortgage officer deter you from a zero-down deal.

- Qualifications for W2 earners vs. 1099 earners are very different with the tax return issue.

- Self-employed file true income and deal with taxes by abatement or amendment.

- Seek and you'll find the right program/lender/CU who will do 100% financing for both your home and any investment property.

Now that you have gotten qualified and know where to get your financing, the next chapter you will learn how to start shopping for a home and be taken seriously as a buyer to get the house(s) you want and negotiate with your seller to pay closing cost.

Chapter Three: Get That House!

If you can, you should, and if you're brave enough to start,
you will.

– Stephen King

We as humans have been negotiating since day one with our mothers for milk, as toddlers for toys, teens for independence and as adults for jobs and relationships. Buying a home is not much different. We'll need to gather some documents from our lender before we go out shopping.

The Pre-Qual/Pre-Approval Letter

Now that we have qualified ourselves, we can go to the bank/lender/CU with confidence to apply and ask for a general pre-qualification/pre-approval letter that states how much you qualify for so that you can show sellers that you mean business and to take you seriously. You'll attach that pre-qualification letter to your offer when you submit your purchase offer to your realtor or directly to the seller's agent if you're doing it yourself.

When submitting your offer this will be the first thing they look at, and the pre-qual letter answers the primary question if you're qualified to purchase the home. They'll want to know the lender and maybe some details about the loan, so the letter satisfies their curiosity a bit. The letter must also be attained before the offer on the home because it covers most of the question's sellers/realtors may have.

Most lenders don't mind issuing them, but be sure to ask for a general letter that can apply to multiple properties if need be so you don't need to chase down your loan officer for each home you want to submit an offer too, which may be a lot. It would be good if the letter indicates the maximum price amount that you qualify for. It should NOT contain the exact details your loan like the 100% financing because we don't want the selling realtor's enthusiasm to go out the window. You should be able to go over this with your loan officer at the bank.

At the end of transaction, money is money whether it came from a loan or from labor income.

Terms for Your Home Purchase 'Offer'

Here I will cover the key elements in the actual purchase contract that will get your offer into escrow with a property you're in love with. When you are submitting an offer to a seller, it should be in proper form. If you're doing this yourself get a current approved real estate purchase contract that realtor's use in your area. It's easy to get a blank one online or get one from a realtor.

If your using a realtor be sure to inform them exactly how you want the financing portion of your offer filled out. This is the most important part of the offer, so don't let a realtor tell you how to do this part as they are working for you not vice versa!

Remember we are thinking out-of-the-box and some of our purchasing terms may seem unconventional to stuffy realtors, so we don't want to give all the exact details of our financing on the purchase contract. Besides, the section where you fill out the financing terms on the written offer change many times anyway and are really arbitrary to a mortgage bank when it comes to funding the purchase.

Financing Section of Offer

In the purchase offer document you'll be asked about your financing. This is the most important part of your offer, the part that will make you look good for the seller is the financing portion on the 1st or 2nd page of the purchase contract. This is where you inform them of your financing terms with your mortgage bank. Granted, like I mentioned these financing terms are totally subject to change and have no bearing on actually funding your loan. The mortgage company doesn't consider that portion of the contract as anything pertinent. It is strictly the seller and their agents who want to see a big down payment because that's the general consensus and to some degree that makes their life easier.

So, when drafting the financing portion of your offer, go ahead and offer to pay the seller's full price, because you're about to initiate a give and take with them that will save you a ton. But before that, first you *must* make yourself a desirable buyer in the eyes of the seller and their agents, especially if there is other buyers' competing on the house you absolutely want. Showing all your cards (loan terms) on the offer is like showing your cards too early on a poker table.

Most 100% loans are frowned by the selling party for no real good reason, other than the seller wanting the security of knowing you won't cancel or fall out of escrow because of the money. People with big down payments fall out of escrow all the time too, so the concern is really unfounded in the hyped illusion of wanting to work with someone who has tons of cash to throw at them. It's just not realistic for most people, our financial system has both rich and poor in a pinch with cash! Plus, why use it if you don't have to?

How we'll present and share our loan terms with the seller in order to make it palatable is to hold the actual cards close to your chest.

Most 100% loans are 80/20, an 80% first and 20% second mortgage. Go ahead and make sure that you *only show the terms of the first mortgage and indicate that you will be putting 20% down from a private personal source.* They don't have to know where or how that will work out. But it's the truth, you're just showing it from a certain angle to make it more palatable. This automatically subtly indicates that you are putting down 20% cash, but remember this is arbitrary to the loan, it's only to emotionally pique the interest of the seller.

Escrow Deposit

Then the next very important move that you write into your offer is what nails it home for the seller to feel most comfortable and to actually choose you: Put a substantial amount in escrow. This is not to be confused with a down payment, this is just a good faith *refundable* deposit to show you mean business.

How much is substantial you ask? Perhaps 2-5% of the home price you got to kind of feel out the situation based on how many other people are trying to buy or how much you really want that particular house. Not to worry though because this deposit money comes back to you at funding when you get the keys or if there's a cancellation within 30-45 days. (You can ask any escrow officer, it's very difficult to lose any money on an escrow deposit, it usually always gets credited back to you even if the deal is canceled by either party.)

Closing Cost Covered

What about the closing cost expense? Loan fees and points etc., can be very pricey.

Here's the important closing cost secret that will allow to get all your escrow deposit money back without paying any closing cost out of pocket: **banks will allow the seller to pay your closing cost up to 6% of the loan amount**. This is what you can negotiate! Therefore, you can ask the seller in the 'special terms' of your offer to pay up to 6% of closing cost. Which can go towards origination and other fees but more importantly, _discount points_ to buy down your interest rates to the lowest available rate possible.

This saves you tons of cash over the course of the loan, literally many, many tens of thousands of dollars will be saved by getting a better interest rate. This can give you a lower monthly payment than a rental or someone who bought at the same price but paid a big down payment and closing cost out of pocket. You will also accelerate your payoff time to lightning speed compared to most homeowners, which I will cover in the last chapter.

Using your savings here to make a refundable deposit in escrow is smart because your 100% loan funds and seller contribution of 6% come in at closing, the deposit and sometimes more will come back in a check from escrow. **The larger upfront good faith escrow deposit on your dream home will sway the seller in your direction even though you get that money right back at closing**. It's really just a peace of mind thing for the seller and their realtors which will work to your advantage when asking for the seller to pay your closing cost.

Chapter Summary

Realtors frown a bit on 100% financing, so you have to finesse them because at the end of the day they are getting the money they bargained for. The bank doesn't care and the seller doesn't care as long as they get what they agree upon.

- Get a good pre-qual letter from your lender that shows the amount you can qualify for

- Offer full price, but you're asking/negotiating up to 6% for closing cost and rate discount points for a super low monthly payment.

- Show 80% financing on your offers with 20% down from a personal source, unless you're asking them to carry back on an investment property through COGO financial.

- Put a big deposit in escrow to sway the seller, you get it back when the deal funds in 30 days or if it is cancelled

In the next chapter you'll learn how to take your new mortgage and pay it off in record time, then how to use the equity value of your home to invest in more real estate.

Chapter Four: Payoff that Mortgage With ZERO Interest

The most important quality for an investor is temperament, not intellect... You need a temperament that neither derives great pleasure from being with the crowd or against the crowd.

– Warren Buffett

A dark fact about the Latin word - mortgage; when directly translated it means 'death pledge'. I've often wondered why the choice of words for this noun, but regardless of the word etymology. I have a good feeling that it's partly because of the interest on a mortgage loan scheduled for the payoff in 30 years will actually be yield a bank almost triple the amount you initially borrowed in profit. The bank would make an astounding 200-400% income off of your monthly payments over 30 years, almost condemning you to a life of slavery for bank profit.

Even with an amazing monthly interest rate, you still will pay up to an astounding 100% more for your home by the time you pay it off because of the APR, which is a different rate usually hidden or glossed over. The monthly and annual interest is what keeps people truly enslaved to the bank.

It's an agreement that basically has a tremendous power over people's whole lives and is quite frankly intimidating and can be overwhelming without the right knowledge. So, please remember the old myth as depicted in American folklore in the song 'The Devil Went Down to Georgia' or like in the film 'The Crossroads' and many other stories where the human being has a battle with the devil. When you go into a home loan agreement you are truly making a deal with the devil himself and you have to be smart or get laid to waste.

But what is little known about a mortgage payment is that it can be paid off in no time through several strategic simple methods. We'll talk about a few of those concepts now and see which one would work best to have your mortgage paid off in a fraction of time with a fraction of the cost. I'll say that these methods are simple but not easy, it requires a reliable income and the mind to understand what is truly happening with your mortgage interest and payments.

How to Get up to 0% Interest on a Mortgage

Earlier we covered how to buy down your interest rate to the bare minimum using the seller's money for discount points. Here we take the saving a big step further to put the banks profit on your loan next to nothing compared what they usually get. I want you to truly understand that interest is not your friend and if left without a thought will sneak in and take all your wealth. It's the like a disease in our monetary system meant to keep the banks in control of all the money and us just trying to keep up.

You know when you get a credit card there is a way to avoid paying interest if you payoff your balance before the interest in compounded on your balance. This concept is very similar except that the balance is much bigger, but the principal is still the same.

The weekly/bi-weekly/daily payment is a concept that works on autopilot from your bank account and can save hundreds of thousands on that nasty interest. The method is somewhat well-known, and you may have heard of it. But I take it a step further than what is usually talked about by bringing in daily payments too.

In today's economy where many self-employed people are paid more often than traditional pay schedules from a job, it's not far-fetched for one to have a somewhat reliable daily income. Of course, that may be a small percentage of people, as most are paid weekly or every two weeks (bi-weekly) and self-employed people can be all over the map.

How ever often it is you get paid, take a percentage of that income to cover just a piece of the mortgage.

If its daily, then a $1/30^{th}$ of your mortgage payment is auto paid by you to the mortgage company to get the ultimate zero interest. If it's weekly, a quarter of the monthly mortgage payment goes to your mortgage account to chop the debt weekly. If you get paid every two weeks, then a half mortgage payment goes to the bank to hack the interest away bi-weekly. If your paid in lump sums as a self-employed person, don't just pay once a month, you can schedule these daily payments for your accounts too by simply allocating it and making the effort.

Many people already instinctively set the money aside and unknowingly do this but instead of giving it to the mortgage company it stays in their checking account or as cash till the payment is due. Meanwhile the mortgage bank is charging and accruing interest on your account *daily* trying to make you pay 3x more for your house in interest fees.

Therefore, with this type of payment schedule, daily, weekly or bi-weekly payments are guaranteed to be a quick fix against the 200 to 300% profit banks usually get on homeowners from daily interest charges.

The payment works by setting up a free autopay from your bank account to disburse a portion of your mortgage every day, week or every other week. So, your total agreed monthly payment gets divided into 2 or 4 weekly or 30 daily payments. This will cut off the interest from accruing and your 30-year mortgage can be paid off in 5-10 years!

You're not changing the amount, your changing the schedule to intercept the daily interest charges. Because this is what makes homeowners struggle, the daily interest accrual. So why not stop that by paying daily if you can, weekly or bi-weekly is great too. Depending on your pay schedule or cash reserve, the more consistent small payments you can make to the bank then the more you stop the compounding interest. Of course as I mentioned daily payments would get you paid off the fastest at 0% interest.

Use A Negotiable Instrument to Satisfy Your Mortgage

This is a way off the beaten path for most people and seems far-fetched but you'll see how we make sense of this. A negotiable instrument in what bankers are used to working with primarily, it is simply a promise to pay a certain amount between two parties. To make it the most simplified it's a I.O.U. In fact, every cash note you have in your wallet unless you're in China right now (because their Yuan dollar is secured by gold held by their govt, not a promise to pay) is a promissory note issued by the Federal Reserve bank or whatever central bank your country is governed by.

The central banks are ultimately the creditor and the government is the debtor who then promises to pay the note in the future from citizens tax payments. This note is what we use as cash. It's also the source of the public debt you hear about. There's no gold securing this money, it is just faith in the government and the power of your labor to pay towards it. Like Charlie and the Chocolate Factories oompa loompas song "All we own, we owe". It's a system secured by debt and labor.

When you sign your mortgage loan at closing of escrow, you sign what is called a promissory note (which in turn becomes the bank note), you also sign a release for the holder of that note (the bank) to sell and trade that note. And they do, the bank sells your promissory note on what's called the secondary market, or the stock exchange where your promissory note is bundled with a bunch other and sold to investors as a mortgage backed security.

When doing this, the promissory document is worth 10x more than what you are already paying because of the charges and trades they can make off of it as a negotiable instrument in security exchanges so in essence it's like cash to bankers.

Many times, the bank collecting your monthly payment has no idea where the note is since it gets traded up to 10 times. You can technically call the bank out on that at any time to check who is the holder of the note, if they don't have it, they legally can't collect on it. However, though very interesting I am not covering that type of legal strategy here. I will cover how to satisfy the mortgage without any lawyers and lawsuits.

Satisfying or cancelling a mortgage is not completely uncommon because of this issue of traded promissory notes, you may hear about it from time to time in the news where a homeowner beats the bank in court over a promissory note and/or a lack of evidence on the part of the bank claiming the right to collect monthly payments or foreclose.

I am not proposing any kind of legal battle with the bank, that would be heavy and risky. Rather this topic covers how to satisfy the bank through other means instead of hard-earned cash. Https://www.cancel1mortgage.info/ is a 10 years old company that has dedicated its whole business to this idea of working with the banks at their own game. But instead of fighting the bank in court or something, which is costly and undesirable for most, they satisfy the mortgage with a new promissory note (negotiable instrument/bank cash) which is then notarized and then sealed with a banker's medallion stamp by any local branch you bank with.

A formal 'Satisfaction of Mortgage' document is then issued to you by the mortgage company to record with the county recorder's office. It's the way bankers create money…

with just a signature and properly formed documents that are negotiable instruments.

The company that provides this service as your personal banker, does charge an upfront fee but I have referred many and have only heard good results.

I have not tried this method personally yet but am very interested because my background in the mortgage industry and knowing how mortgage backed securities work. Look into it and know your options and rights!

Chapter Summary

A mortgage is a big commitment but it's a responsibility that we have and should not be feared so much as to avoid buying. With the payoff methods in this chapter, you will be huge strides ahead of anyone who didn't know these details about the payoff process.

- A mortgage is a contract that can cost you 3 or 4x what you paid for your home, so don't be duped by the bank and use alternative strategies to overcome this conundrum.

- Use daily, weekly or bi-weekly payments to offset the mortgage interest and be paid off in a fraction of the time most will pay.

- Alternative strategies like at www.cancel1mortgage.info/ can skyrocket your situation.

Conclusion:

Billionaire Robert Kawasaki from 'Rich Dad Poor Dad' always advises folks to never sell their homes or property because it's guaranteed to rise based on historical trends. It will always be of value for human beings who need shelter and a place to call home.

Your home is a real estate investment and an asset that will yield a long-term fortune that is accessible for other investing in whatever your heart desires. Now that you know strategies that will beat the bank's curse of the 'death pledge' to pay outlandish interest fees, you can borrow mortgage money with a sense of confidence and accelerate to your dreams.

These methods in this book here are learned after 24 years in the homebuying industry. This knowledge will give the opportunity to use some or all the options available to make homebuying much easier through truly zero out of pocket financing. With this bit of non-traditional, out of the box thinking you're well on your way to successful homeownership which comes with tons and tons of benefits!

Special Thanks

I would like to thank my wife and five children for inspiring me to reach deep down into manhood and provide as only a man can for his family. I would also like to thank all my clients in the past who have walked with me in this process of learning and allowed me to help them on their way to the dream of home ownership.

Also, I'd like to thank the folks at Amazon Publishing who have made it easy to get great content and information out to people through such a great medium.

About the Author

Jason Powers is a real estate professional who has bought 100's of properties for himself and clients throughout his long 24-year career using mainly zero down strategies. He has performed his real estate miracles mostly under the radar and has led a very quiet life. He studied and worked with big names like Ty Cohen and Robert Kiyosaki to get content to you. This is his first writing to date, and he looks forward to many more books to come. He has a wife, three children and lives in San Diego, USA. He enjoys surfing, making music and home schooling his children.

www.ingramcontent.com/pod-product-compliance
Lightning Source LLC
Chambersburg PA
CBHW030538220526
45463CB00007B/2886